200 Plus Educational Strategies to Teach Children of Color

by Jawanza Kunjufu

African American Images

First Edition, Third Printing

Front cover illustration by Harold Carr

Copyright © 2009 by Jawanza Kunjufu

Printed in the United States of America

10-Digit ISBN #: 1-934155-19-5
13-Digit ISBN #: 978-1-934155-19-6

100+ Strategies to Teach Children of Color contains more than 100 insights, tips, techniques, and strategies to improve classroom effectiveness. *200+ Strategies to Teach Children of Color* continues the series with 105 *more* strategies for a total of 200+ strategies.

Contents

CHAPTER 1: FRAMEWORK

My mentor, the late Dr. Barbara Sizemore, used to tell me that as an educational consultant, my job was to observe students, teachers, and staff in action, objectively listen to their concerns, and then (and only then) assess the situation and offer insights and strategies to help our children. While I am pleased that my book *100+ Educational Strategies to Teach Children of Color* became a national bestseller, it might be argued that I compromised my mentor's wise approach by offering strategies before gathering all the evidence.

In my own defense, I'll say that for the past 35 years I have worked with schools and school districts from coast to coast. I have observed and interviewed thousands of students, teachers, staff, administrators, and parents. I have conducted independent literature reviews of research by leading Africentric and mainstream thinkers. And I have documented both my primary and secondary findings in more than 20 books. Rest assured that the strategies presented in *100+* and now *200+ Educational Strategies to Teach Children of Color* are based on real schools, real problems, and effective strategies that are working, particularly with underserved African American and Latino students, especially boys and right brain learners, the most neglected student groups in public education.

The most urgent issue in education today is the academic achievement gap between African American and White students. African American and Latino children, especially male children, have a dropout rate in most urban areas that hovers near 50 percent. Our Black and Latino children scored 300 points below White and Asian children on the SAT. There's a three stanine difference between Black and Latino children and White and Asian children on elementary school exams. Our Black and Latino children are about 30 percent of the children in public schools, but they are almost 80 percent of the children placed in special education and less than 15 percent of the gifted and talented children.

I have devoted my entire career to raising awareness of this issue and its many causes, dispelling myths and stereotypes, and offering strategies for success. Yet many educators continue to believe in the inevitability of the gap, and they blame poverty, single parent families, lack of parent involvement, lack of parent educational attainment, how schools are funded, and even genetics.

Clearly we have a problem. We are facing an educational crisis of epic proportions, but those who are charged with improving student performance don't believe the gap can be closed. They have no faith in our children's ability to learn and their own ability to teach. So if a teacher facing a classroom of 30 students doesn't believe she can teach them, her expectations are already at rock bottom, and she will not give them her best. Our children are more than capable of learning and excelling; our teachers need to reacquaint themselves with the population they serve, and they must be open to new strategies and techniques that have proven effective with African American and Latino students. We cannot afford to lose any more children to systemic neglect. We must close the academic achievement gap.

In my book, *An African Centered Response to Ruby Payne's Poverty Theory,* I make the case that while family income does have an impact on academic achievement, it is not as important as the expectations of teachers. Those educators who agree with Dr. Payne's theory will not only have low expectations of low-income students, they will tend to resist any and all positive approaches. For example, if I tell a teacher that increasing time on task improves grades and test scores, she may not believe it if she has bought into the poverty theory. If I offer our multicultural, Africentric SETCLAE curriculum to educators who believe that low parent involvement is the main cause of the achievement gap, they probably will not be open to giving it a chance. If I suggest that more right brain lesson plans will make the learning experience more inclusive, educators who cite low parent educational attainment as the cause of the achievement gap will not be open to change.

For these reasons and more, I simply cannot wait any longer for teachers to quit looking at the income of the home, the number of parents in the home, parent involvement, parent educational attainment, or school funding. So at the risk of making another compromise, I am offering an additional 100+ educational strategies in this book to help children of color.

The 5 Types of Educators

Unfortunately, the strategies presented in this book will barely register with many educators. As I've mentioned in my previous books, there are five types of educators: Custodians, Referral Agents, Instructors, Teachers, and Coaches.

Custodians are basically the babysitters of the group. As long as students don't cause too much trouble, that's fine with them. Custodians have the mindset, "I have mine, and you have yours to get. I have one year, four months, three weeks, two days, and then I'm going to retire."

Referral Agents aren't much better. Research shows that 20 percent of the teachers are making 80 percent of the suspensions and referrals to special education.

Instructors believe that they teach subjects, not children. Research shows that from the fourth grade on, Black and Latino scores decline. Interestingly, from the fourth grade on, the number of Instructors increases.

My strategies are more effective with Teachers and Coaches who not only understand subject matter, but they honor the congruence between pedagogy and students' various learning styles. You do not teach the way you want to teach. You teach the way your children learn. If you have a large percentage of right brain learners in your classroom, you don't give them left brain lesson plans, i.e., ditto sheets and textbooks. Moreover, Coaches know that you cannot teach a child you have not bonded with. Children learn best when their relationship with Teacher is strong and positive.

In my consulting practice, I've been blessed to observe hundreds of Master Teachers. The goal of *100+* and *200+* is to replicate the successes of Master Teachers in classrooms across the country. Master Teachers have a gift, and many see teaching as a ministry. They arrive at 7:00 in the morning, and they leave at 5:00 in the evening. They take work home with them. They even take children home with them. It's a way of life.

While I commend these teachers, I'm aware that not every teacher is going to devote as much time and energy to the cause, nor should we expect that of every teacher. Teachers are people, too. They have spouses, children, and family responsibilities. They have second jobs, other activities, and other vocations. So it's unrealistic and unfair for us to expect that every teacher is going to give 60 to 80 hours a week to teach Black and Latino children. However, that does not mean they are any less effective.

I've observed that Master Teachers tend to avoid the teachers' lounge. In low achieving schools, the most negative room is not the classroom. It's the teachers' lounge. Making derogatory statements about your colleagues, students, and their parents is not acceptable in the teachers' lounge or anywhere else. Teachers will sometimes tell me that they do not make derogatory statements about Black and Latino children, so they are not part of the problem. But if you do not refute negative comments made in your presence, then you have just become part of the problem. Unless your teachers' lounge is an information center with books, magazines, articles, research, and other documents that will help you improve the performance of Black and Latino children, then avoid this room.

Just as teachers talk about students in the lounge, the students talk about you on the playground. You have a reputation, and you need to know what students think about you. Students are very quick to share with each other what they can and cannot get away with in your class. For example, they may call a teacher "hard" or "nice." "Hard" teachers tend to have high expectations of their students. If you listen closely, they'll talk about this teacher with a little fear and a lot of respect. A "nice" teacher is the last thing you want to be. Curiously, students will sometimes say, "Teacher is nice. He doesn't care what we do." Children are not yet wise enough to know that teachers who don't care are *not* nice. Students say "nice" teachers give away free A's. This is an easy class, which means the teacher has low expectations of the students. Learn the code of the playground, and you'll learn a lot. Principals, if you want to know what your students think of their teachers, listen and learn.

I want you to think about this next statement very carefully: If you have never been on fire regarding the education of your children, it will be impossible for you to burn out. That's prophetic. In my travels, I encourage Master Teachers to relieve stress in healthy, positive ways so that they won't burn out. It has always puzzled me how so many of our best teachers (the Teachers and Coaches) burn out, but seldom will you find a Custodian, Referral Agent, or Instructor burning out. They reason they don't burn out is because they have never been on fire.

I know it hurts Master Teachers to pass on their students to Custodians, Referral Agents, and Instructors. After having worked so hard to raise your children's test scores, I know it disappoints you to have to give them to a teacher who may not be qualified to continue the progress you've made with your students. Try to convince your principal to loop your class from one grade to another. Work with your principal to see if you can loop your children for several years.

More Than A Teacher

Yes, you're more than just a teacher. The role of public school teachers has evolved over the years because the need is so great in our communities. I'd like to add to your job description, but trust me, these functions will make your job much easier.

Motivation. Most teachers in college education departments were trained to work with the *Leave It To Beaver* children and the *Father Knows Best* children. These children come to school already motivated. They've bought into the middle-class value of long-term gratification. But many Black and Latino children, especially those from low-income homes where the father is not present, need motivation. Teachers today must go the extra mile to motivate their students. This can be as simple as a kind, positive word every day. It's tremendously difficult to educate an unmotivated child for 180 days. But when a student is motivated, learning and teaching become a joy.

Home Training. In my book for children, *A Culture of Respect*, I discuss the need for home training. Many of our children lack the basic components of home training. They often disrupt the class and undermine time on task. It is very difficult to teach when students do not know how to behave in the classroom.

Make sure that you are armed and ready with discipline and classroom management strategies (I offer several in this book). Enforce these strategies consistently and fairly.

The Mission

As in *100+,* this book offers practical things teachers can do every day to help their Black and Latino students improve academic performance.

Before we begin, I'd like you to take a moment to think about your African American students. Are they suffering from Post Traumatic Slavery Disorder? How do they feel about Africa? Do they feel Tarzan is the king of Africa? Do they see Africa as the Dark Continent?

How do they feel about dark skin, short curly hair, thick lips, and a broad nose?

Do your children use the B word or the N word? Do they associate being smart with being White?

Do they believe their history began in 1620?

Do they know about the contributions of Dr. Martin Luther King? He died more than 40 years ago, but many of our youth have no real appreciation or understanding of what he stood for. It will take an extra effort on your part to make Dr. King—and all African American historical figures—real.

Do your students believe they're better in sports than science? Do they believe they're better in music than math? Do they believe they're better in rap than reading? If so, your children are suffering from Post Traumatic Slavery Disorder. If you are an African American teacher and believe these things, then you too are suffering from this disorder. If you're White and believe these things, then you're suffering from racism and White supremacy. These disorders must be addressed before you can implement the strategies contained in this book.

We've all heard the phrase, "All children can learn." I want to raise the ante on this idea.

Rather than saying "All children can learn," I want you to believe that your children *will* learn. There is a tremendous difference in using "can learn" and "will learn." I believe in your classroom. Your children *will* learn!

Lastly, I'd like to offer the following words of wisdom:

You can't teach what you don't know.
You can't nurture what you don't love.
You can't respect what you don't understand.

Now we'll move into the heart of *200+ Educational Strategies to Teach Children of Color.*

CHAPTER 2: BONDING

1.

The first day of school is the most important day of the school year. This day will determine who's in charge of your class and how your students will relate to you. Introduce yourself. Let students know you're a human being, but balance that with a no nonsense approach to academics. Let them know that you're expecting great work from them and that you'll be working hard to help them succeed. Explain why the class is so important. In fact, explain why education is so important. With our children, the value of education can never be overstated. Day one lays the foundation for the entire school year, so use it to establish a positive tone.

2.

How soon can you remember all the names of your students? How soon can you pronounce their names correctly? Master Teachers learn all names and pronunciations within the first two days of school. In contrast, it takes some teachers four to five months to learn their students' names, and even then they're still having difficulties with the names. There's nothing more demoralizing to a child than to be an unknown entity in the classroom, and that occurs when the teacher cannot remember his or her name. We all love the sound of our own name, and when an authority figure has taken the time to learn it, this makes us feel important. If you're worried about remembering the correct pronunciation, write the name phonetically and practice saying it out loud on your own time. If you don't learn the child's name, he will talk about you on the playground, and he won't respect you in class. This preparation at the beginning of the school year will establish a positive relationship between you and your students.

3.

Compile a list of all of your students' birthdays. Birthdays are special to children. It's the one day of the year that belongs solely to them. Acknowledge each child's birthday on that particular day. You don't have to give a gift, but you can have the class sing a song or play a game—any creative activity that honors the child in a fun way. Let's make each child important, and birthdays are a great, personal way to do that.

CHAPTER 3: MOTIVATION

4.

Let's take advantage of the Obama Effect. When Barack Obama became the nation's 44th president, our children learned that they could do anything they put their minds to do. Many of our children are now saying that they want to be president of the United States, but it is not enough to say they want to be Barack Obama. They need to understand what this man went through to get to where he is today. Explain his educational journey to your students:

Punahou High School Columbia University	graduated with honors majored in political science
Harvard University	magna cum laude, 1st African American editor of The Harvard Law Review

The story of Barack Obama is highly motivating, and teachers can use the Obama Effect to inspire their children to do their homework, study for tests, improve their grades, and participate in class. And don't forget to put a picture of Barack Obama in a place of honor in your classroom.

5.

The Obama Effect includes First Lady Michelle Obama. Tell your students that before becoming First Lady or even Mrs. Obama, Michelle was an attorney at a major law firm in Chicago. Growing up, she was an outstanding student. She recently said, "I remember there were kids around my [Chicago] neighborhood who would say, 'Ooh, you talk funny. You talk like a white girl.' I heard that growing up my whole life. I was like, 'I don't even know what that means but I am still getting my A.'" That quote alone should dispel our children's belief that being smart means acting White.

The foundation for Mrs. Obama's many accomplishments was laid with high academic achievement. Explain her educational journey to your students:

Whitney Young High	graduated with school honors
Princeton University	magna cum laude
Harvard University	magna cum laude

Michelle Obama left the law firm for a career in public service because she believes strongly in giving back to the community. Use this fact to motivate your students to go above and beyond their normal school work. Encourage them to raise money for worthy causes, join a scouting group, tutor their peers, help around the house, and volunteer at a local community center or church. Use the Obama Effect to motivate your students!

6.

On the first day of the first week of school, give each student two sheets of paper: one, a mock high school diploma, and the other, a mock college degree. The diploma should read as follows:

HIGH SCHOOL DIPLOMA
[SCHOOL NAME]
STUDENT NAME
SIGNATURE   DATE

The college degree should read as follows:

COLLEGE DEGREE
[SCHOOL NAME]
STUDENT NAME
SIGNATURE   DATE

Have students print the high school or college they want to attend, their names, and then sign and date. Higher education is the goal. Remind students that they should never lose sight of the goal. Talk to them about the value of education. Collect the papers and then post on a "Scholars Wall." A table containing college brochures, scholarship notices, etc. can also be placed in this area.

7.

There's nothing more motivating to students than to see their work prominently displayed around the classroom. Decorate your classroom with your students' papers. Change the decorations on a regular basis. During Open House, watch as your students show off their work to their parents. By the way, this is highly motivating for parents, too!

8.

Many schools reward and give more attention to athletic achievement than academic achievement. We need to turn this around. We need to award academic achievements over athletic achievements. Also, we should do this from an African frame of reference. In European culture, I is more important than we. In African culture, we is more important than I. If the student moves from a D to a C, he should receive an award. If he moves from a C to an A, he should receive two awards, and so on. With this system, every student has a chance to receive an award. This is extremely important.

If you only acknowledge one or two students at an awards ceremony, this leaves most students without any recognition. Furthermore, Black and Latino students will stigmatize and ostracize them by calling them "nerds" or "geeks." But if there are many students receiving awards, then just maybe academic achievement will no longer be stigmatized by the Black and Latino peer group.

9.

If you've been teaching for awhile you know that from time to time, there will be a student in your class who seems absolutely resistant to your every effort to teach and manage the class. Whether a learning disability or a behavioral issue is the cause, the student seems driven to disrupt the lessons at every turn. The easy response is to give up on the student. That is what Custodians, Referral Agents, and Instructors do. But I urge you, don't give up on your most difficult students. Refuse to let them slip through the cracks. Unfortunately I cannot give you a simple formula to help such students.

Each student is unique and requires unique solutions. Assess learning styles, emotional strengths and weaknesses, family challenges, etc. This is where your innovation and creativity as an educator must shine through. Even if you are not successful the first few times, eventually you will be successful. Just never give up!

10.

Give awards to your students for perfect attendance and perfect punctuality during the week, month, or year. It doesn't have to be an expensive gift. Simple certificates, stars, stickers, books, pencils, etc. will be much appreciated. In addition to giving awards to individual students, you can give awards to learning teams or gender-based groups. Stress the benefits of attendance and punctuality in achieving academic and life goals.

11.

Motivating students to take tests can be quite a challenge. Educators often feel forced to teach tests and subjects, not students. As a result, students are apathetic about their lessons. They are not curious or mentally stimulated by the lessons. They often do not understand why a particular lesson is being taught. All they know is that they better memorize the facts for the test. Maybe if we thought of a test as a review of the material rather than some overwhelming, frightening life-or-death activity students wouldn't feel so intimidated by them. There's so much pressure on both students and teachers to meet state and federal standards that the joy of learning is too often lost. Realistically, the tests must be given, but perhaps our attitude about them can change. Tell students that you're going to use the test results to improve your own teaching. Tell them that the tests will be used to provide feedback on student (and teacher) strengths and weaknesses, which will help the entire class to improve. Master Teachers and Coaches know how to channel fear, anticipation, and even dread into excitement, anticipation, and a positive can-do attitude. Build confidence for test taking. Rather than calling it the "state exam" or "standardized test," call it a game. Give awards to the group (cooperative or single gender) that has the best score.

12.

The word "can't" is not acceptable in your classroom. Teach students that can't is like a curse word. Leverage President Obama's campaign slogan: YES I CAN!

CHAPTER 4: YOUTH DEVELOPMENT AND SELF-ESTEEM

13.

You can use the power of your position to broaden the horizons of your students. Many of our children believe that the entire world is contained within the borders of their neighborhood. They know little about how different groups of people live beyond the community. One way to expose students to how different people live is to take them on a field trip to the wealthiest neighborhood in a 25-mile radius of the school. This will stimulate new thoughts about what's possible in their own life.

14.

Take your children to the finest university located within a 25-mile radius of the school. Let them visit the dormitory and talk to students and professors on campus. Visit the Student Center, library, science labs, and lecture halls. Make sure each student takes home brochures and a course catalog. As a homework assignment, have students study the catalog and then write about a course of study they'd like to pursue in college. Make sure they include the different subjects they'll have to take.

15.

Eating together is an excellent way to spend time with family and friends. Unfortunately our children bond at fast food restaurants and junk food vending machines. African American neighborhoods are full of unhealthy eating establishments, but there are virtually no health-oriented or five-star restaurants. A creative and fun field trip would be to take your students to a quality restaurant outside of the neighborhood. Expose them to fine cuisine, healthy meals, and exotic international dishes. Talk to them not only about the menu, but show them the proper way to behave at the table.

16.

Your students may never have been exposed to office buildings, banks, and the municipal seat of government. Too many only know about the currency exchange, pawn shops, the mall, and the police station. An excellent field trip would be to take your students downtown to visit the commercial district: banks, corporate offices, and City Hall. This is the engine that drives the city, so talk to them about whatever interests them: the flow of money, prominent careers, different retail outlets, cultural centers, real estate and architecture, etc. Have them write about their experience and what they learned.

17.

Our children can learn a lot about dignity and self-esteem from Asian cultures. For example, never embarrass a student in your class. African Americans may not call this saving face, but it's the same idea. Asian peoples have a reputation for being hard workers, and they have extensive social rituals for treating others with respect. Teach students about the positive rituals and attitudes of various Asian cultures. As a classroom activity, have students create their own respect rituals— for other students, for teachers, and for parents. For example, have students practice bowing to one another. It is difficult to be disrespectful when you greet a peer with a bow.

18.

Have students repeat the following chant first thing in the morning or right after lunch (when energy levels sometimes slump):

I am Black (or Hispanic), beautiful, and smart.

I can achieve whatever I desire.

I promise, you will read about me in the future.

Remember, I am Black (or Hispanic),

beautiful, and smart.

19.

1 06 & Park is a BET program that features music videos and interviews with leading hip hop and R&B artists. There are a couple of ways that you can use this program in your classroom. First, watch it and learn about the music and culture your children most enjoy. This is where they live. Their values, fashions, music and dance choices, and speech are inspired by programs like *106 & Park*. Second, show a video of the program and have the students try and detect if there are any African American females with dark skin, short, natural hair, and wearing a modest style of dress.

Discuss why they probably won't see this image of womanhood on a music video. This issue is extremely important regarding the self-esteem of African American females and the sexual perspective of African American males.

20.

Your students can learn a lot about the importance of having a positive attitude if you tell them the old Christmas story about the twin brothers. As the story goes, one boy received lots of toys for Christmas, but he broke them all. The other twin was given a room full of horse manure. Without even the slightest complaint, he dug through the manure. He refused to have a negative attitude, and as a result, he found a $5 million pony. Which boy had the more positive, productive, beneficial attitude? This story is sure to stimulate a lot of animated discussion, but make sure students discuss the importance of having a good work ethic and a positive attitude.

CHAPTER 5: BOYS

21.

Whether playing a game of football or playing the dozens, boys love to compete, and they love to win. This is not a bad thing. It's simply the way boys are, and we need to do whatever we can to leverage their love of competition to improve their academic performance and close the achievement gap. Whenever possible, create single gender groups. Single gender competitions will reduce disciplinary problems and improve academic achievement. Competition will inspire boys to close the gap between female and male achievement.

22.

Offer recess in class. In my book Keeping Black Boys out of Special Education, I discussed how many children, especially boys, are being placed in special education because of their high energy levels. This could be addressed if we simply provided them with opportunities to release some of their energy. Since so many elementary schools in low-income communities no longer offer recess, we must begin to think of other ways to let boys run around and jump up and down. One way is to use exercise as a disciplinary method. If a student acts out, instead of him taking a "time out," have him do several jumping jacks or push ups.

23.

Almost 80 percent of boys in special education are there not because of ADD or ADHD. They're there because of a reading deficiency—and that can be improved if attention is given to the problem. Black and Latino males tell me that the books in their classrooms and school libraries are BORING! I've heard this so often that I would be remiss if I didn't encourage you to purchase books that will appeal to boys. Remember, boys like to read about cars, sports, hip hop, science fiction and they love comic books. Put yourself in the shoes of a Black or Latino male. Look at the books in your classroom and school library through their eyes. Honestly, are these books entertaining to your male students? Ask your male students what they think. Males in general love to give their opinions about everything, so use this secret to male psychology to get them interested in reading. Please visit our website www.africanamericanimages.com under new releases. The set is called best motivational books for boys.

CHAPTER 6: PEER MENTORING AND STUDENT LEADERSHIP

24.

All children have special gifts, and a little recognition will go a long way in developing their self-esteem and confidence. Identify your best students, and empower them to become tutors. If possible, provide them with a small financial incentive or extra credit points. Incentives will encourage more students to improve their academic performance and become tutors. This is also a powerful way to develop positive peer relationships, empathy, and leadership skills.

Make sure to provide an orientation or training for tutors. Offer the following guidelines:

1. Tutoring is a big responsibility, so take it seriously. Tests can be won or lost based on how well you do your job as a tutor.

2. The goals of tutoring vary with each student. You may need to help a student master a subject or prepare for a test. Make sure you know the needs of the student before beginning.

3. Time on task is all important. Do not allow anyone to distract you. Make sure cell phones are turned off.

4. Do not judge. Just because a student needs assistance doesn't mean that he or she is "stupid."

5. If you don't understand something, ask your teacher for help. Never ever "wing it."

6. Maintain a positive attitude when working with students. Always be encouraging, and give praise when it is due.

25.

One way to ensure that homework assignments, tests, and quizzes are returned to students in a timely fashion is to turn over the work of grading papers to students. Students will receive double if they catch the checker doing something incorrect. Not only will you have a checker checking the work, but when the papers are returned to the students, the students review the checker and if there are errors, then the student will receive additional points.

26.

The Obama Effect can open students' eyes to possible careers in public service. Many of our children are now saying they want to be president of the United States, which is good, but they must learn that you don't become an elected official on a hope and a wish. You can't just turn 35 years old one day and decide, "I'm going to be president." The process of preparation takes years, and it sometimes begins by serving in student government, even as early as elementary school. Create a student government in your class with an election and officers. Student government teaches children how to work together, organize, manage, and brainstorm campaign issues. By running for president, vice president, secretary, or treasurer—or by managing a campaign—students will begin to develop the work ethic, public speaking skills, organization, and management skills needed to run a campaign and serve their fellow students in office.

Public service is also a journey of self-discovery. Students will discover their own opinions and beliefs about various issues. Public service empowers students by showing them how political science can be applied to the real world.

27.

At least once a week, have your class participate in a community service project. Whether cleaning up the neighborhood of debris, visiting an elder at home, working in a soup kitchen, or working with the physically challenged, our children must learn the importance of community service.

By the way, having children clean up the neighborhood will encourage them to not litter in their community.

28.

Letter writing campaigns serve multiple purposes in leadership development. Writing letters to customer service departments, elected officials, the media, etc. teaches students to take responsibility for what happens in their community.

Have your students write letters to President Barack Obama to let him know how they're doing in school. They can also ask him to visit their classroom. You never know: he just might show up!

Students should know the following before beginning this letter writing campaign:

1. How to properly format the letter.

2. What information must be included in the letter—name, date, school, classroom, teacher, etc.

3. How to properly address President Obama.

4. How to correctly spell his name.

5. Making sure grammar, punctuation, and spellings are all correct.

6. Handwriting should be neat.

7. Paper should be clean.

29.

Have students write a letter to First Lady Michelle Obama. Since she is the First Lady, the contents of this letter should be different from the letter to President Obama. For example, since Mrs. Obama is passionate about community service, supporting military families, the arts, and education, students can write along these lines. And by all means, have students ask her to visit their class. See strategy #28 for letter writing tips.

30.

Encourage your male students to consider attending a college or university that develops both leadership skills and academic excellence. Morehouse College in Atlanta, Georgia, is the only Black male college in America. Teach your children that HBCUs (Historically Black Colleges and Universities) only have 12 percent of the student population but produce 30 percent of the graduates. Seventy-five percent of African Americans who go on to White graduate schools graduated from HBCUs. Have pictures of Morehouse posted on the walls of your classroom. Show pictures of African American male students. Also, if possible, during spring break, take your students, especially males, to Morehouse.

31.

Spelman College (Atlanta, Georgia) and Bennett College (Greensboro, North Carolina) are the only Black female colleges in America. It is important for your female students to be aware of the strengths and excellent reputation enjoyed by these two colleges. Not only do African American women receive an outstanding education at these institutions, they receive more personal care and attention than they would at a large university. When they graduate, young women are fully prepared to lead in their chosen careers, or they go on to enroll in higher education programs. Spelman and Bennett are two stops definitely worth making on your HBCU field trip.

CHAPTER 7: LEARNING CAPACITY

32.

Not only do many students have a short attention span, the entire country has a short attention span. Our food comes from fast food restaurants, drive-thrus, microwave ovens, and vending machines. We have become addicted to the ease and speed that iPods, cell phones, texting, and emailing provide when communicating. Thus it should come as no surprise that children can't sit still for long periods of time during class. If you give a 50-minute lesson plan to a student who has a 22-minute attention span, you will not be effective. Consider shortening your lessons, or break them up into smaller time segments.

33.

Research has shown that boys perform better mentally when the classroom temperature is cool. The ideal temperature for boys is 69 degrees. Boys may be overheating when they keep their jackets on (a hip hop style), so make sure that jackets and hats are off. The ideal temperature for girls is 76 degrees—however, if it gets too hot, everyone in class will go to sleep, especially after lunch. What is the temperature in your classroom? Lowering the temperature even a couple of degrees might be difficult to implement, but still, talk to your principal or building engineer to see what can be done.

34.

One day each week, put the textbooks away. Many of our right brain learners do not do well with textbooks. They learn better by talking, listening, drawing, handling artifacts, or just moving around. Not only will your students enjoy the change of pace, you, too, may enjoy the challenge of teaching old lessons in new ways.

35.

Go one day a week without using ditto sheets. I believe that interesting facts about science, math, and history were never intended to lay flat and lifeless on a ditto sheet. No wonder our children are bored. Shake things up in your class. Wean yourself from your ditto sheet dependence. In our high tech world, content is being adapted for all types of formats, from digital downloads to audio CDs. So find other ways to deliver your lessons. Your students might find learning fun for the first time.

36.

It has been said that as age increases, creativity declines. Allocate time for art, dance, or music activities—especially art. Too many of our children have underdeveloped art skills. We must encourage students to express themselves through drawing and painting. This develops new neural pathways in the brain and boosts our children's innate genius.

Do your students a favor and allow at least five minutes a day for creative activity. Let them write in a journal, sing a song, write a rap, or draw a picture. Creative activities can also be connected to the day's lessons. Have students write a math poem or create a DNA collage. One creative first grade teacher had her students draw their self portraits as an African mask. She said the colorful final products were as fine as any authentic mask from Africa. She posted them on the walls outside of her classroom for the entire school to see. Another idea is to have students create self-portraits as Egyptian pharaohs and sphinxes. Our children need to see themselves as royalty, so this activity has the added benefit of boosting self-esteem. The possibilities are endless!

37.

Every once in a while, challenge students to invent a new thing. We often think about creativity in terms of art or music, but inventing is also a highly creative activity.

One way to approach this activity would be to present a technical or mechanical problem that needs fixing or a need that must be met. It can be as silly as a new way to roll toilet tissue or as serious as a new method of conserving energy or going to the moon. The goal of this activity is to challenge students to think and dream out of the box and beyond what they think they're capable of. So even if the ideas are unworkable or strange, don't block the flow

of creativity by being negative or making fun.
You never know what one of your students may
dream up one day!

38.

Make sure every lesson has a visual component. Black and Latino children tend to be right brain learners. They need more visual stimulation than a textbook or a ditto sheet can provide. In fact, all children will appreciate "seeing" the lesson rather than always having to read it.

39.

Another way that visual learning can be incorporated in the classroom is by videotaping student speeches, oral exams, general student participation, and assemblies. Imagine if an argument or fight was caught on video and was then played back for the benefit of those involved. Video feedback can also be used positively, to reaffirm a student's good work. If a static picture is worth a thousand words, then a video is worth a complete story. Video feedback can be invaluable to students and should be used to improve performance and enhance self-esteem.

40.

Make sure that every lesson has an auditory component. Our children listen to hip hop because they enjoy the words set to music. It's curious that more teachers don't leverage this widely known fact. Use every opportunity to deliver your lessons as auditory activities. For example, reading a book while also listening to the book on tape is a highly effective way to improve reading comprehension. Also, the dramatization and music often included in audio productions make reading an enjoyable activity. The goal is to encourage students to become readers for life.

41.

Make sure that every lesson has a kinesthetic component. It's not natural for children to have to sit still all day. No wonder they're fidgety and climbing the walls by noon. Once upon a time recess and gym gave students the opportunity to burn off excess energy, but today in many low-income communities, such programs have been cut.

Some of our children learn best when they can move—boys especially. It may get a little noisy, but occasionally let children get up and move around. Better yet, incorporate movement into your lesson plans. Nearly anything can be memorized while dancing, exercising, walking, climbing, running, skipping, jumping, spinning, marching, and wiggling. Why not let children learn the way they learn naturally?

42.

At least once a month do not give students a written exam. Give a right brain test where students will either have to draw the information, demonstrate with an artifact, or talk (oral exam).

Whenever I make this suggestion to teachers, the response is usually, "How do I quantify this approach with a grade?" Perhaps the answer is to create a different type of rubric where different intellectual and behavioral faculties are assessed. One of the most powerful findings to come out of intelligence research in the past couple of decades is that there are many different types of intelligences and that all are valid in helping us understand the world. Yes, state and federal standards must be met, but never lose sight of the fact that you must educate the whole child, not just the left brain of the child.

43.

Before discussing the geography of the nation and the world, have students explore the geography of the classroom, school, and neighborhood. Children should know the directions of their classroom: east, west, north, and south. When you go out into the hallway, ask children if they know which way (direction) they're going. Which way (direction) is the cafeteria? The principal's office? The girls' and boys' rest rooms? The playground?

Take students on a mini field trip: walk around the school grounds. Have children point out their directions. Tell them to point to their homes and various neighborhood landmarks and name the directions.

44.

Cooperative learning builds learning capacity while making peer relationships more positive and academics-focused. Class distractions, negative perspectives about scholarship, and risky behaviors are usually caused by negative peer dynamics. Cooperative learning activities offer teachers the perfect opportunity to influence peer dynamics and to improve academic performance *together*.

Do everything you can to incorporate competitive activities (spelling bees, math contests, debates) into the lessons. Teams can be comprised of cooperative learning groups and single gender groups. Have students name their teams and even design their own tee-shirts or wrist bands for group identification and pride.

45.

Children love to touch things. It's one of the many ways they learn about the world. Place in your classroom as many objects as possible that they can touch and that will stimulate their curiosity—pets, plants, building blocks, movable words. Unfortunately, as children get older, they ask fewer questions. Children are born curious, but then something happens to make them more cautious about expressing their curiosity. So make sure that you're constantly on the lookout for artifacts that will stimulate your students' curiosity.

46.

My career as a public speaker began in my freshman year in college when I joined the debate team. Debating is an excellent way to develop verbal, analytical, and critical thinking skills. Students learn to think quickly and on their feet as they form thoughtful responses to points made by the opposing team. Your "dozens" players may be the stars of this activity, while other students will have to work through their fears of speaking in public.

Although debating appears to be a lot of arguing back and forth, there is an art to it. There are rules. Students learn how to present their views without shouting or being verbally abusive. They must learn the art of persuasive communication. Hopefully, this skill will cross over into peer relationships, and students will use their debate skills to resolve conflicts peacefully.

Create debate teams, and have students debate various issues. Single gender teams have tremendous potential for bringing out strong opinions. Have students watch *The Great Debaters*, a wonderful movie based on a true story (directed by Denzel Washington).

47.

I'm a huge advocate of journal writing for young people. This is an excellent way to teach students to communicate using the written word. In our Information Age, the ability to write one's thoughts clearly is a necessity. English teachers often use journal writing at the beginning of class to warm up and jumpstart the writing process. You can do the same. During the last five minutes of the day, have students write about what they learned in class. Or, you can keep this activity open ended by letting them write whatever they want; however, they may have trouble getting started.

Providing ideas can help reduce comments such as, "I don't know what to write about." On the other hand, your star writers might enjoy the freedom to choose their own topics. Since this activity is about increasing confidence with the written word, be flexible, and don't fret over grammatical or spelling mistakes. Hopefully, by the end of the school year, journal entries will get longer, the writing will flow more easily, and students will no longer fear the blank page.

48.

When we were growing up, we had to stand up in class whenever answering a question. Today, students remain seated, and many never participate in class discussions at all. Fear of public speaking is a problem with students (and adults). We need to address this as early as possible in the educational experience—as early as kindergarten and first grade. To make children comfortable speaking publicly, make speaking a part of the curriculum. When answering questions or making comments, make sure students stand up first.

49.

Getting your students involved in a journalism project is an excellent way to develop research, critical thinking, and writing skills. Develop a class newspaper, and have students conduct research and interviews and write articles. Have them interview peers, teachers, the principal, school staff, parents, family members, neighbors, and prominent members of the community. They can write about interesting facts they learned in school. They can even write commentaries about local, national, and world events. Help them develop a "nose for news." Make sure you get your artists and digital photographers on board as well. Have students take pictures and draw political cartoons.

A creative use of this journalism project would be to do a historical newspaper set in another place and time. As an Africentric project, this is a powerful way for students to appreciate history because they'll have to get into the heads of historical figures and events. How about The Underground News Report, featuring news all along the Underground Railroad? The possibilities are endless!

By the way, parents will enjoy the fact that their students' works are featured in the class newspaper. This is an excellent way to strengthen the parent-teacher relationship.

50.

Perhaps in no other subject is the academic achievement gap more glaring and disturbing than reading. African American and Latino students trail far behind Whites in reading scores. According to The Nation's Report Card (2003, National Assessment of Educational Progress), in reading, 12 percent of African American fourth graders and 14 percent of Latinos are "proficient," whereas 39 percent of Whites are "proficient."

Too many of our older students, especially those who have been retained, are reading at very low levels. They are embarrassed and bored by the *Dick and Jane* type reading materials they have to read in middle school and high school. Help your students improve their reading skills without damaging their self-esteem by purchasing high interest, low skill reading materials. Visit the African American Images website under new releases where we list high interest, low skill motivational book sets for boys and girls.

51.

Reading comprehension is not necessarily connected to speed or the ability to read aloud. Too often we connect reading aloud or reading fast with comprehension and accuracy. For right brain learners, reading is about creating the images while reading. While left brain learners are more comfortable reading aloud and reading fast, that's no guarantee that their comprehension is the best.

Provide a reading experience for right brain learners where they can read quietly and at their own speed. This will allow them to create their own mental images. If you'll allow this approach in your class, you'll be pleasantly surprised as their reading comprehension improves.

52.

In most inner city schools, reading activities have become an urgent priority. Likewise, we must increase the quality and quantity of writing assignments for students. Not only are many of our students challenged by reading, they also lack writing ability. Try to allocate at least 30 minutes or more a day to writing book reports, essays about a lesson just learned, etc. The more students write, the more comfortable they'll be with the process.

53.

Reading Is Fundamental is not only the name of an organization; it's the truth. Reading is the most important subject students must master because all other subjects depend on it. Encourage your student to read books, not only for school assignments but for pleasure. And make sure that with every book they read, they write a report summarizing what the book was about. This will strengthen comprehension, and it will also let you know which areas require improvement. In many of my previous books I mention the story of the African American surgeon, Ben Carson. When he was a boy, his mother made him go to the library, read books, and write reports. I tell his story a lot because it is so inspirational. He went from a virtual failure in school to one of the most respected surgeons in the world. Have your students read his autobiography and write a report.

54.

Our children need to understand that teaching a slave to read was once illegal in this country and that their ancestors fought and shed blood for the privilege. Talk to your students about how much Frederick Douglass loved to read. He loved to read so much that during slavery, he would sneak out to try to read. Often he was caught and beaten, but he continued to read. On a good night he would read under the stars. On a bad night he would read by candlelight. He loved to read. Every time he read he would say to himself, "There must be something about reading, books, and an education that some people don't want me to have." That motivated him even more to read every book he could get his hands on. Once you are educated, the knowledge you've acquired can never be taken away. Teach your children the significance of Frederick Douglass and his love of reading.

55.

Talk to your students about how much Malcolm X loved to read. While he was in prison, he read almost every book he could put his hands on—including the dictionary! He literally read the entire dictionary, from A to Z. Once Malcolm was released, he never went back to jail. He always said it was because of reading. He was exposed to good information in books.

Malcolm's story is especially important given the fact that some governors determine future prison population rates based on fourth grade reading scores. They are well aware of the fact that low reading ability is a risk factor in incarceration. As I've documented in my books, African American male scores tend to decline from the fourth grade on, and they have the highest incarceration rates. Teaching our boys to read is a matter of survival, and they need to understand how important it is. Malcolm's prison experience puts the plight of today's African American male in the perfect context.

56.

Since our children are so entranced with money, we can use it to improve their math scores. As much as possible, connect educational concepts to money, and physically use the money to teach the concept. Many of our children learn best when they are able to actually touch, play with, and manipulate artifacts, so allow them handle play coins and dollar bills. To add to the fun and excitement, store the money in an old treasure chest (or have your best artist paint a box to look like one).

The following are some activities that will help students master simple math concepts:

1. Have students count the number of coins and dollar bills as well as their total value.

2. Teach children how to make change.

3. Have students solve word problems using money.

57.

It's unfortunate, but students learn very little about their own bodies. One of the best science lessons you can offer students is to teach them that the body is made up of 103 minerals, nutrients, and vitamins. This makes science relevant to their lives. Every day they should eat foods that are rich in these minerals, nutrients, and vitamins. It is disappointing how students can have elementary, high school, and college degrees but know nothing about the relationship of the number 103 to the health of their bodies.

58.

Periodically, set aside time for a Technology Hour. Discuss the Internet, gadgets, new websites, new forms of technology, and where technology is going. For example, Japan is on the cutting edge of robotics. In fact, they are pioneering having robots actually teach students. Ask your students how they would like being taught by a robot. Will robots eventually replace teachers one day? This will probably be a lively discussion, but let them talk.

One of President Obama's initiatives is to reduce our dependence on foreign oil and increase research into new energy technologies. Have students draw pictures of their homes with windmills or solar panels. Also, every year MIT holds a solar car race. The cars look very space age, and the students will enjoy looking at pictures of the cars or videos of the race. Have them design or even build their own idea of what a solar car could look like.

Children are so fascinated with technology that they may be able to teach you a few things.

CHAPTER 10: CLASSROOM MANAGEMENT

59.

Our children need to be held accountable for their own classroom performance. Develop a contract for your students, and have them complete and sign it at the beginning of the year. Feel free to use the following:

> I __STUDENT NAME__ will try to be present and on time every day. I will try to participate every day. I will try to complete all class work and homework on time. I will try to study as much as I can. I will try to do my best on quizzes and tests. I will strive to be an A student.
>
> _____
> Signed
> _____
> Date

When students fail to meet their responsibilities, show them the contract they signed. Remind them that their word is their bond.

60.

We all know that rules should be introduced on the first day of class. But how many teachers actually engage their students in the rule making process? If students help make the rules, hopefully they won't be so quick to break them.

On the first day of school, present your rules and post them in a visible place. Next talk to your students about the importance of rules in the classroom. The goal is to make sure that the teacher and students are all respected. That means no name calling, cursing, or violence. Moreover they are to respect the educational process. That means no sleeping in class and always coming to school prepared with supplies and homework completed. That also means participating in open discussions in a respectful manner.

Next ask students for their input. What rules would they like to see on the board? Feel free to ask guided questions about their commitment to academic performance and excellent classroom behavior to jumpstart the discussion.

61.

Have you ever thought about putting a suggestion box in your classroom? This is an excellent way to get students' thoughts about issues they care about, and the suggestion box also allows for anonymous input.

Setting up a suggestion box is simple. Just get a box big enough to hold several cards, and cut a slot on the top. Place blank index cards next to the box. Students can write suggestions anonymously and place them in the box. Encourage your students to take advantage of the suggestion box, but explain that the purpose of the box is to improve the classroom experience.

Disrespect is unacceptable. This will teach students how to take responsibility for the quality of their educational experience.

62.

One of the main reasons why minor conflicts escalate into major events is because teachers often play favorites. To enhance the management of your classroom, make sure you're consistent and fair with your students. One of the greatest compliments students can pay to a teacher is, "She's tough, but she's fair." Don't play favorites. Think of the referee at the basketball game who misses the infraction but sees the reaction. As a result, he makes a "bad call," and the coaches, players, and fans protest loudly.

If a conflict arises in the classroom, solicit input from not only those involved but the bystanders as well. Try to get an understanding of what happened from multiple points of view. That way you won't jump to conclusions. You don't want to be known on the playground as the teacher who plays favorites. Always be fair.

63.

Consider carefully how you want your students to sit in your classroom. Master Teachers do not let students randomly sit where they want.

On the other hand, when creating your seating chart, consider arrangements other than traditional rows. If your class size is small, why not have students sit in a circle or horseshoe formation from time to time. If your class size is large and the room is small, you may not have a lot of options, but still try and have students face each other sometimes. This changes the entire mood of the room from status quo to "there's something different going on." That enhances engagement and bonding and reduces boredom.

64.

Put student supplies in a central location in the classroom, and keep them in the same place. Children love to waste teachers' time. One of the ways they do this is to say that they don't have a pencil or pen, crayons, scissors, paper, or a book. Master Teachers stay on task—they stay with the lesson, they point to that central location in the room, available and accessible, where students can secure whatever materials they need.

65.

Allow at least three to five minutes at the beginning, middle, or end of the day to let students express some of the challenges they are having in class. The rule is, "Everything we discuss stays inside of the room. We are family." This is an excellent practice in classroom management because it can prevent conflicts and problems from arising and escalating.

It's very important that your classroom feels like a family. Teacher, you are the mother or father. The students are your children and siblings to one another. During this meeting time, constantly stress that "family members don't fight. We stick together. We encourage each other."

CHAPTER 11: DISCIPLINE

66.

Sometimes even the best classroom seating plans don't work. Talkative students are placed side by side, or a boy can't stop talking to a girl because he has a crush on her. That's easy enough to fix: just separate the students. But what if a child refuses to be quiet or won't stop throwing spit balls?

Custodians, Referral Agents, and Instructors will send the student to the office. Master Teachers will figure out a way to resolve the situation. When I was a student, teachers would have students stand in the corner, facing the wall. They believed in isolating, ostracizing, and humiliating students. While this approach may have temporarily addressed the problem, it didn't get to the underlying issue of why students needed to "act out." There are many complex reasons, but sometimes the simplest answer is the right one. Students may be *desperate* for attention from Teacher, the consistent day-to-day authority figure in their lives.

A Master Teacher will sense this, and she will have a disruptive student sit right next to her desk for awhile. That way she can keep an eye on him, and the student gets the attention he craves. Master Teachers are creative. If one approach doesn't work, they'll try another. Sending students to the office is a last resort.

There's a relationship between your proximity and the problem. If you want to reduce disciplinary problems, make sure you are close to where those problems are taking place. There really is a science to where children sit and where teachers stand.

67.

My grandson's kindergarten teacher used a very effective disciplinary strategy with her students. Feel free to adapt it to meet the needs of your class. She used an easy-to-recognize color system. If the children did well in school, they received a green light. If they received one or two warnings, they received a yellow light. Any more than two warnings, they received a red light.

My wife and I found this system really helpful because it was so easy to understand. All we had to do was look at the color in our grandson's folder and we'd immediately know how he had behaved that day. The system made monitoring his behavior easy. So whenever we asked, "Son, what's your job?" he would say, "Bringing home the green lights!" It was an excellent way of shaping behavior.

68.

Children will often say that their major problem in school is not algebra, geometry, or physics, not biology, chemistry, or English. The greatest problem is bullying. When it comes to dealing with bullies, teachers are sometimes caught between a rock and a hard place. School policies regarding how to handle acts of violence may leave children feeling vulnerable. You may want to protect the child, but you're not able to.

Students will only tell you what's going on if they trust you. You must find a way to provide them with protection. Many of our students have not been confident sharing their most intimate concerns with educators because they've seen how students are not protected when secrets have been divulged.

69.

School policies around violence and bullying seldom address prevention. Before bullying gets to be an unmanageable problem in your class, resolve to prevent the problem in the first place. Do not allow bullies to get a foothold in your classroom. You must take authority. Begin by identifying all the bullies in your classroom. Pull them over to the side and help them understand how their bullying is really broadcasting to the world their weaknesses—their insecurities and low self-esteem. Terrorizing peers is a sign of weakness, and they must understand that.

Next organize the class into a "no victim zone." Teach students that they have more power as a group than the bully does by himself. Sometimes in order to save themselves, students will side with the bully, which robs the group of its power. Talk to the class about the low self-esteem of bullies and how their actions are really a cry for help. Help transform student victims into victors.

70.

Never let a student sleep in your class. It disappoints me to see a student disengaged and sleeping with his head down on the desk. Look at those students as if they were your own biological children. Would you want your child to be sleeping in class?

Talk to the parents about their child's behavior. Together, try to find out the cause. Maybe he's not getting enough sleep at night. Or maybe his listlessness is symptomatic of a deeper medical, emotional, or addictive problem.

71.

One effective way to prevent discipline problems is for students to have lunch in the classroom instead of the cafeteria. Teachers say that having so many students of different age ranges in one room is a recipe for disaster. One way to correct this problem is to offer lunch in the classroom. Tell students, "We're family, we eat lunch together, we have a good time together." This makes lunchtime a more intimate bonding experience. Play jazz or classical music softly in the background. Teachers, this is a great time to laugh and joke with students. Tell them funny stories, or ask the students if they've heard any good (clean) jokes lately. Let your class clowns do stand-up. You can even discuss good nutritional habits during this relaxing time together.

72.

Cheating is unacceptable, and throughout the school year you should constantly stress students' responsibility to study so that cheating is unnecessary. Students only cheat if they haven't studied or if they lack confidence. Stress the value of education. Getting good grades is wonderful, but learning the lesson is far more important. We've stressed test scores and grades so much that I think we've all lost sight of the goal of education: to learn.

Some teachers create a test environment where cheating is impossible. They allow open books and calculators. There are times, however, when this will not be possible—during standardized tests, for example.

During the test, do everything within your power to discourage children from cheating. Stress at the beginning of the test that cheating will be harshly penalized with a reduction in scores and a note to parents. Make students show that their hands and arms are free of notes. During the exam, do not sit at your desk and grade papers or walk out of the classroom as so many teachers do. Walk the aisles during the test. Constantly scan over the heads of the classroom for talking and unnecessary movements. And if you catch a student cheating, make him feel the pain so that he will never cheat again.

73.

Do not nag your students. If your rules are posted prominently in your classroom, then the foundation for discipline has been laid. Give students one warning. If they do not respond, then simply tell the student, "I want you to stay after class, and we will discuss the issue." But you do not need to nag your students over and over again. It is not fair to your other students, nor is it fair to you. Nagging is ineffective with students, and after awhile they stop hearing you.

74.

Students need your attention, some more than others. In fact, students who act out usually need your attention the most. While positive attention is preferred, unfortunately some will settle for negative attention. For these students, negative attention is better than no attention at all. One of the best ways to handle attention seekers is with praise. Try to give three times more praise than criticism. Hopefully this will influence attention seekers, especially class clowns, to realize that when they are positive, with you they can receive what they want more than anything else: attention.

75.

The next time you're confronted by an angry student, try this three-step approach:

1. Have him tell you why he's angry. Listen without judgment.

2. Affirm his right to his feelings.

3. Give a smile, a word of encouragement, or a hug.

This approach works well because it is hard to stay angry when someone is smiling at you. Kindness diffuses the pain, and sometimes students just need to know you care.

76.

Most disciplinary problems are created by student conflicts. All their lives, students have been exposed to poor modeling of conflict management in their families and communities, and so they only demonstrate what they know. Teach your students how to manage conflict so that physical fighting is no longer the inevitable outcome. Talk to them about the difference between battles and wars. Battles are conflicts you would like to win, but if you don't, life goes on. A war is a conflict you must win. It's a necessity. Tell them that it is better to lose the battle and be around for the war. Many of our students make critical mistakes because they expend all their energy arguing and fighting over battles, which leaves them unavailable for the war.

CHAPTER 12: TIME ON TASK

77.

When are your students at their mental and behavioral best? When are they the most academically engaged? This is very important information because we want to do everything in our power to help our children succeed in school. Consider giving your quizzes and tests during the hour when you've noticed that your children are at their best. Is it the first hour? The middle hour? The last hour? There may even be a day of the week when students are alert and ready to learn. Is it the first day of the week? The middle of the week? The last day of the week? When planning your next quiz or test, take this valuable information into consideration.

78.

I devote a lot of attention to time on task and timing in general because our time with students is limited, so we must maximize every moment to improving academic performance and overall youth development. In one of my earlier books I mentioned the 555 Rule. This rule is simple and elegant and doesn't require any training to master. Simply, the first five minutes and the last five minutes of the day are critical, so pack these precious moments with high impact activities. Use the first five minutes (Prime Time) to set the tone for the day. When students finish early, be prepared with additional challenging work for the last 5 minutes.

79.

I'm a real stickler for time on task, and taking attendance should never take time away from instruction. Master Teachers know that there's a correlation between how much time is given to instruction and academic achievement. You'll never see them taking time away from the lesson just to take attendance. That's a waste of precious time. Attendance can be taken at any point during the class period. For example, you can quietly take attendance when the students are completing an assignment.

80.

Intercom announcements are a notorious time waster. It would be great if you could turn off the intercom, but even I will concede that it is needed for emergencies and communication with teachers from time to time.

Ask your principal to eliminate the announcements that are made over the intercom. If your principal is unwilling to completely eliminate the announcements, see if you can negotiate for a reduction. Lobby for only the most important announcements being read over the intercom once or twice a week— but definitely not every day.

81.

Students are very clever. They know that if they "act out," you'll stop teaching to deal with the disturbance. Dealing with discipline issues steals time away from teaching, and that's not fair to students who want to learn. Try to minimize discipline while teaching. Unfortunately many teachers are losing time on task because they're spending more time disciplining students than educating students. Address discipline issues during recess and lunchtime and after school. When a problem arises, simply tell the student, "I will discuss that with you later." Or you could make a quick change to a seating arrangement.

82.

When a student arrives late, do not take the rest of your class off task. It is a terrible waste of time to stop teaching just because of one late student. Be prepared for dealing with late students. Point to where the work is, have the paper on the desk, have the student come up quietly when you're not teaching—but do whatever you can to not allow the one late student to disrupt the entire class.

One way to prevent tardiness is to give a quiz or an assignment as soon as students walk through the door. If they miss the assignment because of tardiness, deduct points or give them a zero.

83.

We can think of time on task in many different ways and in many different arenas other than school. Once acquired, this skill will help students in every area of their lives. Time on task helps prevent procrastination. When time is limited, time on task focuses the attention on whatever needs to be done.

Teach your children the importance of time on task by discussing the accomplishments of African American heroes. For example, rap artist Tupac only lived to 26 years of age, yet seven CDs have been released after his death. Tupac used his short time on earth in a highly productive, focused way. Martin Luther King was only 39 years old when he was assassinated, but while he was alive he changed the world in a short amount of time. The lesson from Tupac and Dr. King is not about how long you live; it's about what you do while you're here and how well you manage your time.

CHAPTER 13: HEALTH

84.

In most of my books I discuss the fact that African American and Latino children tend to be right brain learners. Many thrive with visual and auditory instruction. Now imagine these two faculties wasting away simply because medical attention was neglected. Then the child is diagnosed with a "learning disability" that could have been prevented all along.

Many school districts offer students visual and hearing exams. When this service comes to your school, make sure parents are aware and make doubly sure that each one of your students is tested. If your school does not provide and you feel a child needs an exam inform your principal. Our goal as educators is to help every child succeed academically, and one way to do this is to provide medical assistance for the children who need it.

85.

One of the greatest tragedies to hit public schools in the inner city is the cutting of physical education programs. Gym has been reduced to a throwaway class of 20 to 30 minutes a week. In some neighborhoods, elementary schools are being built without playgrounds. And then we wonder why there are so many problems with childhood obesity and discipline in our schools. Our children simply are not moving around enough. They need gym every single day.

If your school has cut back on gym, instead of seeing this as a negative, let's view it as a positive opportunity to redesign the curriculum. Since the attention span of our children is short anyway, use exercise to break up the lessons. Every 20 minutes or so, stop the lesson. Have students stand up, stretch, do jumping jacks, run in place, etc. By the way, don't just tell them, do the exercises with them. Teachers need movement, too!

86.

Sexually transmitted diseases are at crisis levels in the African American and Latino communities. One of every two Black or Latino girls has an STD. Forty-three percent of all males who have AIDS in America are Black and Latino, and 69 percent of all females in America with AIDS are Black and Latino.

Believe it or not, you can influence the lives of our girls and boys. First, they are too young to be even thinking about having sex, so start there. Talk about the benefits of abstinence. Make science and health class relevant to their own bodies and sexual behavior. Some of our children have never heard the abstinence message, so they don't even know it's an option. Tell both males and females that not only is it possible to say no, it is preferable. In math class, discuss the financial realities of STDs and unwanted pregnancies.

Some progressive middle schools and high schools hold single gender afterschool rap sessions. Anecdotal evidence suggests that with excellent adult facilitation, these sessions can be very supportive and very effective.

CHAPTER 14: CREATIVE TEACHING

87.

Think about all the times you had to take a professional development training. Now think about the workshops you couldn't wait to leave and the ones that were truly enjoyable. Chances are, the workshops that were the most fun had a lively facilitator, interesting information, and engaging activities.

Our children are no different. It is difficult for children to sit still all day long and listen to boring, monotonous, monotone lectures. That's why so many of our children "act out." They are bored silly. Could it be that you're bored, too?

You may have a standardized curriculum to deliver, but there's nothing stopping you from having a good time with your students. Make lessons fun and entertaining. Whenever possible, infuse games into the lessons, or transform the entire lesson into a game.

88.

Exactly what is a credit score? Do you know how the system works? Our children need to know because their future financial self-sufficiency will depend on it. This is critical for Black and Latino students who come from low-income families. An understanding of credit and financial responsibility could mean the difference between poverty and self-sufficiency.

Children see their parents using plastic, and they think the credit card is, literally, money. Only as they become young adults will they be able to think in the abstract and realize that the credit card is used to secure loans. And loans must be paid back. If the loan is paid back by the monthly deadline, the credit rating will be good. If not, the rating will be bad. Good credit ratings mean that you don't have to pay as much for things. A bad credit rating means that you'll have to pay two or even three times as much for things.

Good credit ratings can be a tool in building wealth. It is very difficult to build wealth with a bad credit rating.

Teach your students about importance of credit and credit scores, and you will have laid a powerful foundation for their future financial responsibility. Begin teaching students as early as kindergarten.

89.

You're never too young to learn how to create a budget. If students receive an allowance or have a part time job, budgeting is a skill they must develop, and you can help them.

The traditional budget will look at how much money is coming in and how much will be spent on expenses (utilities, clothes, food, mortgage, etc.) Teach your students about budgeting at a level they can understand. Start with two categories: *needs* and *wants*. Right now they think all their wants (expensive gym shoes, video games, CDs, etc.) are needs. They must learn the difference. Needs are about basic survival: food, *basic* clothing, shelter. Wants are about entertainment. The responsible approach to money management is to pay debts, save, pay for needs, and then spend on fun things—not the other way around. They should also learn to give some of their money to help someone in need.

Students must learn that managing money well will help them build wealth in the long run. Mismanaging their money will lead to debt and poverty. Teach them that if they don't get a handle on their needs and wants, they'll end up spending their every penny on things they don't really need. The goal is to lay a strong foundation for financial self-sufficiency and responsible money management.

90.

Keep up with hip hop culture. At least once a week, watch MTV and *106 & Park* (BET). Listen to rap CDs. Check out hip hop fashions and dances. Hip hop is a global movement, and it has a tremendous influence on our children. To understand the mindset of Black and Latino children, teachers must understand what hip hop is all about.

Also, use hip hop culture as a creative teaching tool. Try the following ideas:

1. Analyze themes in rap lyrics.
2. Write a rap tune.
3. Bring in a plain white tee-shirt (costs $5 at the beauty supply store). With paint,

have them "tag" their name in a creative, colorful way.

4. Research and write a report on a famous rap artist.

5. Challenge classroom debate teams to battle (no profanity!) about an issue.

6. Older students can write a paper on the value system promoted by hip hop. Have them compare and contrast the negatives and positives of "bling bling," "keeping it real," "no snitching," etc.

91.

We are finding that even young children can learn simple algebraic concepts. Like reading, algebra is fundamental to math fluency. Algebra is nothing but solving for the unknown and recognizing patterns and quantitative relationships (through identifying, categorizing, and sorting). The earlier we teach algebra to children, the better. Mastering even the simplest concepts will give students confidence.

If your older students are struggling in algebra, use the approach of the kindergarten teacher: use artifacts to teach algebraic concepts. The more they manipulate the artifacts, the deeper the concepts will sink in. **I encourage you to read our book How to Teach Math to Black Students.**

92.

Why a second language is not taught as soon as children enter kindergarten is beyond me. The research is consistent. If a child is taught a second language in the early grades, chances are he will become fluent in that language. Teach a second language as early as kindergarten. If there is no formalized language program at your school, try and sneak some lessons into the school year. Teach students phrases in several foreign languages. There should be 10 to 15 different phrases in several different languages that you can share with your students. If there are students in the class who speak multiple languages, have them share a few words (numbers, colors, etc.).

94.

Enthusiasm will go a long way with students, so be enthusiastic about teaching. It doesn't matter if you're teaching physics or phys-ed, students will become interested in your subject if you teach with barely contained excitement. They may make fun of you, but deep down they'll love you for "keeping it real." Master Teachers know that enthusiasm is contagious. If you are not enthusiastic about the lesson, your students won't be either. Do everything you can to be energetic, up tempo, exciting, and enthusiastic with your students.

95.

When you take a day off from school, how smoothly does your class run without you? Are you confident that your students will continue to learn? Do they get their work done? Are they on their best behavior? Or when you return do you find that absolutely no work was done, and reports of bad behavior greet you the moment you clock in?

When the substitute teacher first comes to your classroom, does he find a folder that contains the day's lessons and assignments? Or will he find an empty desk? Too often substitute teachers come to a classroom cold, with no agenda, lessons, or assignments to guide the day's activities. The first question they ask students is, "What have you been working on?" They ask this question because the teacher has left no notes, nothing. Imagine coming to a classroom for the first time with no guidance from the teacher. The substitute must figure out a way to keep students busy for the entire period (middle school and high school) or day (elementary school). No fault to them, they often take the babysitting approach of the Custodian.

Given the academic achievement gap and all other challenges facing Black and Latino students, everyday must have learning as the priority. Whether or not you are present, your students must always be learning. For the sake of your students, make sure that you always have a substitute folder. This folder should have at least one to three days of lesson plans for your students. Also, let your students know how they are expected to behave. In fact, include this expectation in your list of class rules.

96.

Sometimes it's the small changes that can make a big difference. Take a look at your chalkboard. Is it clean, or are there old lessons still on the board? One mistake teachers sometimes make is keeping old information on the board for too long. Children need to see fresh information constantly—or else they'll no longer notice the information. Unless this work is crucial and needs to remain on the board, make sure the chalkboard is clean at the beginning of each day.

97.

Your students come to you for the answers to life's major questions. But who do you talk to when you have questions? Teachers need mentors. Forty percent of teachers leave the profession within five years, but this disturbing statistic could be turned around if teachers had mentors to guide them. That's the blessing of having a mentor. They've been there and done that. They can help you navigate the challenges of teaching and help you to become the best you can be. They'll tell you what you're doing right and what you can do to improve.

Identify the best teachers in your school, and observe and shadow them. Unless your teacher's lounge has a positive, supportive atmosphere, I would not recommend that you seek out mentorship there.

98.

One of the complaints I hear from students and parents is that they don't receive their work from the teacher in a reasonable amount of time. I've even heard of students not receiving their work at all! This is inexcusable. Students will assume that you don't care about them or their education. Return all quizzes, tests, and homework to students within 48 hours. Using student checkers can speed up the process. Remember, children have a short attention span. They will lose what they learned from the assignment if you don't return it to them within a reasonable period of time.

99.

Sometimes there's just not enough time during the school day to grade papers, write up lesson plans, and complete all the other tasks you have to do. The solution is simple—add more time to the day. Arrive 30 minutes early and stay 30 minutes after the last bell rings. Not only will this help with your time management and organization, you'll be able to devote more planning time to curriculum development, communicating with parents, refreshing bulletin boards, etc.

100.

Teachers get burned out because of stress and boredom. Every year the same lesson plans day in and day out. Yes it will take extra effort to write new lesson plans, but isn't that better than being bored?

Every year, have at least 10 to 25 percent of your lessons be completely new. Teachers often burn out because they teach the same concepts the same way over and over again. Writing up new lesson plans will force you out of your comfort zone. You may have to do research and practice up on delivering your new information.

101.

Do students feel comfortable asking you to slow down? Sometimes children miss key concepts simply because they are afraid of appearing unintelligent. They would rather ask their peers or skip the concept altogether than ask the teacher to slow down.

Master Teachers create a classroom environment in which children feel comfortable in the learning process. The classroom is a safe haven of learning. Students who ask questions are viewed as smart and brave. They are curious, engaged, and they desire to learn. Speeding through key concepts can damage a student's desire to learn. So if a student asks you to slow down, then slow down.

102.

Covering the curriculum or teaching the test is not teaching. That is the approach of Custodians, Referral Agents, and Instructors. Master Teachers don't believe in just delivering information that will last for only a few moments; they believe in teaching students. Do not allow the 180-day school year to be reduced to three or five days of teaching a standardized test. Granted, there has been a tremendous focus on improving test scores and raising grades, especially among Black and Latino students, but we cannot strive for the perfect numerical score while leaving the soul of the child behind.

Do not allow society, your principal, or community to reduce your efforts to simply covering the curriculum and teaching the test. Do not allow yourself to be compromised. You owe yourself more, and your students deserve better.

103.

One of the best ways to learn is to make mistakes. I can sense a massive shudder among all teachers reading these words. But it's true, being a good student isn't about being a perfect genius. It's about having the courage to try out the most difficult concepts, ideas that seem beyond your mental grasp. I love it when Master Teachers have such high expectations of their students that they challenge them with difficult assignments and projects. The students may complain, but deep down they want to be challenged.

When you give your students a really difficult assignment, let them know that at the beginning they will probably make mistakes, but that you fully expect them to master the concepts at the end of the process. What begins as disbelief among students transforms into wonder and then self-confidence as they discover abilities within themselves they never knew they had.

Allow your students some mistakes. Let your classroom be a safe haven so that students are not ashamed or afraid to make incorrect statements or ask strange questions.

Dignify wrong answers with the respect they deserve. Don't let your students clam up because of shame. Make them comfortable with a mistake or two of your own!

104.

Be proactive. You must have strategies in place for as many events in the classroom you can think of. Being taken off guard by various student behaviors can create chaos in the classroom, and it can be difficult to restore order if you're not prepared. Master Teachers have seen it all, heard it all, and they are prepared for nearly every possible event. If a student hollered at you, what would you do? If a student cursed at you, what would you do? If a student attempted to hit you, what would you do? Good teachers are proactive. They know in advance what they will do in many types of events.

105.

What Master Teachers know:

The mediocre teacher tells.
The good teacher explains.
The superior teacher demonstrates.
The great teacher inspires.
If your students are not learning the way you
teach---you need to teach the way they learn.
***How** you teach is as important as*
***what** you teach.*

CHAPTER 16: EPILOGUE

If you purchased the first book in this book series you now have more than 200 strategies to help children of color succeed in the classroom. Early in this book I mentioned that the most urgent crisis facing Black and Latino students today is the academic achievement gap. Maybe you noticed that the strategies contained within this book are constantly urging you, in many different ways, to raise your expectations of your students. Do not allow their family lives or the condition of their community to fool you into thinking that they are not capable of being great student scholars. They are more than capable.

Low teacher efficacy is a problem in under-served schools. I hear the same complaints from teachers over and over—that the parents are not involved, that no matter what they do, Jamal still can't/won't read. Just as I do not accept that our children cannot learn, I refuse to accept that you cannot teach our children. My belief in teachers is high. As long as you genuinely care about our children, even Custodians, Referral Agents, and Instructors can improve. Teachers and Coaches can always do better.

So please keep *100+* and *200+* on your desk at all times. When you are challenged by an event in your classroom, refer to the wisdom contained within these books, for that wisdom came from observing your colleagues in action. These strategies have been tried and tested by Master Teachers—and they work.

School Sets

Black History Curriculum (SETCLAE) 67 BOOKS, teachers' manual, and other products, *(specify grade)*, SEBH . . . $595.00 each
    Educators' Library 22 books, SEEDL . . . $199.95
  President Obama Set of 12 elementary books, 2 high school/ teacher books: Obama Set . . . $149.95
  Children's Library (every children's book in the catalog), Grades K-8, 224 books, SECL . . . $2,179.00
Hip Hop Street Curriculum: Dropout Prevention/Motivation 80 BOOKS and teachers' manual, *(specify grade, grades 5-H.S.)*, HHST . . . $595.95 each
Male In-house School Suspension 50 books, *(specify grade)*, SEM . . . $399.95 each
  Female In-House School Suspension 50 books, *(specify grade)*, SEF . . . $399.95 each
Black History & Cultural Videos (10 Pack, VHS Only), MIV1 . . . $199.95
Hispanic History & Culture 50 books plus posters, HHCV . . . $419.95
Posters Set (230), SECP . . . $399.99 (non-returnable unless damaged)
  Biographies set of 25 Famous African Americans Paperback, BI01 . . . $349.95
  Biographies set of 16 Famous African Americans Paperback, BI02 . . . $159.95
    Parent Set 22 books SECPA . . . $199.95
Math Set 30 books, 3 videos, and 1 game, *(specify elementary or high school)*:
  Elementary: SEMA-EL . . . $399.95 each, **High School:** SEMA-HS . . . $399.95 each
Respect/Manners/Home Training 25 books, RMH-SET . . . $199.95
Best Books for Boys/Girls: Motivational Reading Books for At-risk Males & Females (20 Books), *(specify gender and grade)*: SEMR . . . $299.95
  Character Developing Books for Youth Set (10 elementary books), CD400 . . . $129.95
  Classics Set of 20 famous black books, CL500 . . . $279.95
Complete School Set 520 children and adult books, 20 audios and 10 videos: SCHSET . . . $19,999.99 (offer includes: *7 day "luxury" resort sleeps 6 anywhere in the 50 states*)

Free Shipping! (for a limited time only)
Don't let your grant monies expire.

African American Images, Inc.
P.O. BOX 1799 * CHICAGO HEIGHTS, IL 60412
To Order Call: *1-800-552-1991* * *Fax us at (708) 672-0466* * E-mail us at Customer@AfricanAmericanImages.com
Visit our web site at http://www.AfricanAmericanImages.com

Notes

_____

_____

_____

_____

_____

_____

_____

_____

_____

_____

_____

_____

_____

_____